Tryst

by

Karoline Leach

SERVING THEATRE

S F

SINCE 1830

SAMUELFRENCH-LONDON.CO.UK
SAMUELFRENCH.COM

TRYST is fully protected under the copyright laws of the British Commonwealth, including Canada, the United States of America, and all other countries of the Copyright Union. All rights, including professional and amateur stage productions, recitation, lecturing, public reading, motion picture, radio broadcasting, television and the rights of translation into foreign languages are strictly reserved.

ISBN 978-0-573-11064-1

www.samuelfrench-london.co.uk

www.samuelfrench.com

FOR AMATEUR PRODUCTION ENQUIRIES

UNITED KINGDOM AND WORLD
EXCLUDING NORTH AMERICA
plays@SamuelFrench-London.co.uk
020 7255 4302/01

Each title is subject to availability from Samuel French,

depending upon country of performance.

As the play begins, **GEORGE** *stands, looking out at us. Somewhere in early middle age, dressed in the clothes of the early twentieth century, he is assured, attractive. He stands and looks at us for a while.*

GEORGE. I'm what you'd call a careful person. Organised. I know what I'm after, I know what I want. And I get it. I live on my wits. And my charm. And I do quite nicely. Quite nicely thank you. I have all my suits hand made. No rubbish. I go to the same place as the duke of Marlborough and Lord Asquith. Of course it's expensive. But you have a duty to yourself don't you. I get the looks too. All the women look. They know quality. They know style. I could have any one. Any one. But I pick and choose.

He freezes into immobility in his arrogant posture.

We see **ADELAIDE** *sitting stage l. She wears the clothes of the same period, her hair pulled back from her face. She may be slightly younger than* **GEORGE.**

ADELAIDE. I work in a hat shop off the Edgware Road. I been there twelve years. Twelve years this November. I work in the back room doing the sewing. There's five of us in the back room. Alice Fuller, Mary Lee, Jane Parker with the funny leg. Rose with the teeth. We all got something wrong with us, that's why we're in the back room. Where the customers can't see us. What's wrong with me?

She looks down at herself.

GEORGE. You got to pick with care. Know the signs to look for. It's the face you're looking for. The sort of face that belongs to the sort of woman who teaches piano or serves tea or issues library books. Only that's not all you're looking for. You're looking for the little inconsistency. The little something too expensive, too new, too nice for that face. The something that tells you its got a nice little nest egg. A few quid stashed away.

ADELAIDE *handles the gold pin at her throat.*

ADELAIDE. This brooch was Auntie Myra's. I always wear it. She used to live with us Auntie Myra. And when she died she left me this and fifty pounds. I thought of spending it all on nice things. But instead I put it by. For a rainy day. I got my own little bank account. I think about that money. I think 'that's there, I can use it whenever I like'. I know what I want to do with it. I've done all the sums. I know just what I want to do with it… one day…

GEORGE. You got to know how to use money. I can use money. If I had enough what I wouldn't do.

ADELAIDE. One day… I thought about a holiday, or a whole lot of holidays. I'd quite like to go to Venice. I've got a black velvet skirt I'm saving and a white silk blouse. I could go to Venice and wear my black velvet skirt and my white blouse and float down the canals in a gondola *(she looks down at herself.)* … One day

GEORGE. It's a surgical operation when I do it. This is the way it goes; I see one, size it up. I move in, always watching my back, leaving nothing to chance. Charm it up, act smitten, bowled over. After a few romantic meetings you look into its eyes and ask it to marry you before anyone can stop it. And it says –

ADELAIDE. Yes.

GEORGE. They always say yes. You tell them to bring their bank book on the honeymoon so the name can be changed. They say

ADELAIDE. Yes.

GEORGE. You say don't tell a soul. They say.

ADELAIDE. Yes.

GEORGE. You tell them to take out all their money and give it to you to look after. They say.

ADELAIDE. Yes.

GEORGE. You take the money and bugger off. I tell you, whoever says women should get the vote needs his head examining.

ADELAIDE. Rose says it doesn't matter what you look like so long as you've got good eyes and a good heart.

GEORGE. I've left them all over. I left one waiting for me outside the Gents on Brighton pier.

ADELAIDE. There's someone out there for each one of us, she says, who'll love us for what we are.

GEORGE. Climbed out the back window, by the time she cottoned on I was on a train to Margate with fifteen quid in my pocket.

ADELAIDE. Someone nice.

GEORGE. Mind you, I'm never cruel. I never hurt them. I've never hurt anyone.

ADELAIDE. Someone kind.

GEORGE. And I do give them a good time. I always go through the formality of the wedding night. None of this get it in, get it out and get away. I spend the night with them and make love to them with tenderness and consideration. And I leave them smiling. I take pride in it. I like to think of it as quid pro quo. If you know what I mean.

ADELAIDE. Someone to smile back at me.

> **ADELAIDE** *stands and moves to the back of her chair.*

November 15 1910.

GEORGE. Cold bloody morning. No money. No breakfast. Down to my last ha'penny. Dodged the landlady and went out.

ADELAIDE. Got up a bit late. Frost on the windows. Missed the bus. Got into work ten minutes late. Mrs. Pear shouted… Late again Miss Pinchin and that green hat to finish…

GEORGE. Spent my last ha'penny on a cup of tea in the little cafe by the British Museum. I was hungry. Starving hungry. And looking. Searching the faces. Looking for the signs.

ADELAIDE. I spent the morning doing the green hat. The green hat with the double bow and the ruching. Fiddly work. Taken me five solid days. But by lunchtime it was finished. And it did look nice. I showed Mrs. Pear. She said "good job of work, Adelaide, you put it in the window since I'm off to dinner"…

GEORGE. Pawned my watch in the usual place and took a walk down the Edgware Road, looking into the shops, watching the cabs and carriages. And the fat comfy people inside them. Hungry. Turned down Bell Street to get some soup at the cheap place on the corner.

ADELAIDE. I went into the shop, all quiet and empty. Felt funny being out there, where I'm not allowed. Stopped for a minute to look in one of the mirrors. Don't know why. I hate mirrors.

GEORGE. There was a little sign up over a dull little shop. 'Pear's Milliners of Refinement and Quality.'

ADELAIDE. I put the hat on, just to see. It didn't look how I thought it would. So I took it off quick. I remembered what I was about and went to the window.

They are level with one another, only the 'window' beween them.

GEORGE. Poky little window with a bit of cheap velvet curtain.

ADELAIDE. Pulled back the curtain.

GEORGE. And looked in.

ADELAIDE. He looked at me.

GEORGE. She smiled.

ADELAIDE. He smiled back.

GEORGE. I decided to forget about the soup. And went into the shop.

As she leans into the window he moves behind her and speaks, taking her by surprise.

Good morning.

She jumps.

If I might see the green hat you were putting in the window.

ADELAIDE. Oh. I'll just find someone to help you.

GEORGE. I'd be quite happy for you to serve me if you don't mind.

ADELAIDE. Oh no… I don't deal with customers. I do alterations in the back room. I'm not supposed to deal with customers.

GEORGE. I'd still like you to show me.

ADELAIDE. Mrs. Pear wouldn't like it… I'm not supposed to you see, I wouldn't normally be here, only I was putting…

GEORGE. Just this once won't matter will it?

ADELAIDE. I suppose not, since Mrs. Pear's gone to dinner.

GEORGE. You mean luncheon.

ADELAIDE. Oh yes I suppose I do.

They laugh. They look at one another.

GEORGE. But why aren't you at your luncheon, is Mrs. Pear such a hard taskmaster?

ADELAIDE. Oh no… in the back room we don't go till one.

GEORGE. I see.

She remembers the hat.

ADELAIDE. Here's the hat.

GEORGE. It's very nice.

ADELAIDE. The bows are Belgian lace…

GEORGE. Yes.

ADELAIDE. Three peacock feathers and satin ruching.

GEORGE. Would you permit me to compliment you on the exquisite simplicity of your costume.

ADELAIDE. I beg your pardon?

GEORGE. Please don't think me presumptuous but in this age of vulgar excess I could not help but be struck by your taste and restraint. The single ornament at your throat, the little pearl in your hair.

Quite lovely.

ADELAIDE. Thank you.

GEORGE. No. Thank you – for bringing a little warmth into a cold day.

They look at one another.

And now I must wish you good day.

ADELAIDE. Pardon?

GEORGE. Good day sweet lady.

He turns to leave.

ADELAIDE. But… But what about the hat?

He turns back.

GEORGE. Oh… I'm afraid that was only a pretext. To pass a moment with you. I hope you can forgive me.

He is gone.

ADELAIDE. He was gone.

GEORGE. Leave them gawping. That's the way. Made a little mental note and went to get me soup.

ADELAIDE. I went back to work. Did all the stitches wrong one side of the straw and had to stay late redoing them. Stew for tea. And the ironing to do.

GEORGE. Got home and the landlady's waiting behind the door. With some big bloke she says is her son. They want ten shillings back rent. He's not the sort you argue with so I hand over four shillings. Pretending it's all I've got. Times are hard and I've got a sick sister in Leigh-on-Sea. After a while he lets go of my collar and I slip upstairs and bolt the door.

ADELAIDE. I dreamed one of my dreams. Where the shop bell rings and I look up and there's the Prince of Wales come to take me out to dinner. I'm all lovely and light and laughing – you don't mind if I go a bit early do you Mrs. Pear? And she's there curtseying – oh dear me no Adelaide, do just what you like Adelaide. The whole shop watches and I get into his carriage and wave bye bye and off we go. Me and the Prince. Only this time when I looked at him he had a different face.

GEORGE. Next day I was out in the street before anyone was stirring. Down to the public baths as soon as they were open. Slipped them a dodgy sixpence I'd picked up the day before and pocketed the change. Good soak and scrub. Best silk tie. Bit of scent. Bit of oil. The mark of a gentleman.

ADELAIDE. Went to work as usual. The green hat was still in the window. I looked at it… Did a bit more on the big merry widow hat for Miss Oliphant's wedding.

GEORGE. One o'clock and I was strolling down the Edgware Road towards the corner of Bell Street. Little fish-fryers full of shop girls taking their dinner back to work. That's the one. So I found a doorway a little way from it and bided my time.

ADELAIDE. Out to the fish shop round the corner. Four cod and chips and one plaice.

GEORGE. Saw it come round the corner and timed my walk to perfection.

They come up against one another.

Good afternoon… Again.

Pause.

An extraordinary coincidence.

ADELAIDE. Yes.

GEORGE. But of course – your luncheon hour. Please don't let me detain you… You mustn't keep the fortunate gentleman waiting.

ADELAIDE. Sorry?

GEORGE. I am sure he is very jealous of your time.

ADELAIDE. I'm not meeting anyone.

GEORGE. I beg your pardon.

ADELAIDE. I was just going into the fish shop.

GEORGE. He is out of town then, your gentleman friend.

ADELAIDE. I don't have a gentleman friend

GEORGE. I find that impossible to believe.

ADELAIDE. It's true.

GEORGE. So you were about to embark on a solitary luncheon – and so was I.

Would it seem a great impertinence if I were to suggest that we take luncheon together?

She looks up at him.

ADELAIDE. Oh.

GEORGE. You are offended. I'm sorry, I should not have asked. Do forgive me…

He begins to move off.

ADELAIDE. No… please.

He stops.

I should be very pleased to…

GEORGE. You are so very kind… Miss…?

ADELAIDE. Pinchin. Adelaide Pinchin.

GEORGE. What an unusual and charming name.

ADELAIDE. No not really.

GEORGE. Mine is Love

ADELAIDE. Oh.

GEORGE. George Joseph Love.

ADELAIDE. That's nice.

GEORGE. So would you do me the honour Miss Pinchin?

ADELAIDE. I would be very pleased to Mr Love.

GEORGE. My favourite restaurant is round the corner – shall we walk?

Took her to a place in Oxford Street where everything was in French. Ordered soup with onions and bits of fried bread and half a bottle of the cheapest wine.

They sit at the table.

ADELAIDE. French onion soup and Beaujolais Nouveau.

GEORGE. My usual I said. And smiled at the waiter as if we were old friends.

ADELAIDE. Crème brûlée to finish. And a half a bottle of champagne.

GEORGE. Sparkling wine.

ADELAIDE. He told me all about himself.

GEORGE. I lied. Said I'd been in the diplomatic service.

ADELAIDE. He was fluent in four languages.

GEORGE. And with General Gordon in Calcutta.

She notices the mistake.

ADELAIDE. Khartoum.

GEORGE. Pardon?

ADELAIDE. General Gordon was in Khartoum.

GEORGE. Yes, but he was in Calcutta first. I was attached to his general staff. In a civilian capacity.

ADELAIDE. Really?

GEORGE. Being a fluent speaker of… the native language.

ADELAIDE. Were you shot at?

GEORGE. I should say. By the Mad Mahdi himself on one occasion

ADELAIDE. You must have been so afraid.

GEORGE. All in a day's work.

ADELAIDE. He asked me all about myself, and listened as if I was really interesting. I told him about Auntie and the way she'd gone so quickly with congestion of the lungs…
Carried off in a month

GEORGE. Oh dear.

ADELAIDE. With her knitting half finished.

GEORGE. Oh dear.

ADELAIDE. Still – she left me a little bit.

GEORGE. Oh.

ADELAIDE. Fifty pounds.

GEORGE. Oh.

ADELAIDE. And this brooch. It was her favourite. The diamonds are set in little flowers – see.

GEORGE. How exquisite.

ADELAIDE. And there's a little inscription in French.

GEORGE. Ah yes.

ADELAIDE. I suppose you know what it means.

GEORGE. Oh yes. *Tout Pour Mon Amie* – 'I love Amy' .

ADELAIDE. My auntie's name was Myra.

GEORGE. It's the French form.

ADELAIDE. Oh.

She receives it back from him. She looks at it.

I always wear it. It makes me think of her.

GEORGE. I expect it was given her by an admirer.

ADELAIDE. I don't think she had any admirers.

GEORGE. Then you obviously don't take after her.

ADELAIDE. Oh.

There was gold curtains and painted ceilings. There was a little trio playing waltzes.

We hear the music, soft and distant like a memory.

And we danced.

They do, turning slowly round one another.

He told me about spying for the British Government in South Africa.

GEORGE. More lies.

ADELAIDE. And how his dog starved to death during the siege of Ladysmith.

GEORGE. Nice touch the dog.

ADELAIDE. He told me about his time in Vienna…

GEORGE. Attached to the embassy.

ADELAIDE. And his tour of duty in Berlin and St. Petersburg.

GEORGE. The Grand Duchess Olga gave me a Fabergé egg as a small leaving present.

ADELAIDE. Golly.

GEORGE. Only a small one, but it's the thought that counts. I still have it at home. I have always intended to give it as a keepsake to someone very special. But no one has ever been special enough…

They both stop, looking into one another's eyes.

So far…

They hold the look for a moment more, then he breaks away.

When the wine was all gone I said I'd settle the bill and meet her outside. Skipped to the gents, locked the door and out the window. Then I walked her back to work.

ADELAIDE. I felt light and funny.

GEORGE. We stopped outside her shop and I looked into her eyes. I am very taken with your company Miss Pinchin.

ADELAIDE. Oh.

GEORGE. It would be pleasant to pass another hour with you – some time very soon.

ADELAIDE. Yes.

GEORGE. Dare I hope for tomorrow?

ADELAIDE. I think so…

GEORGE. I will wait for you here – at one.

He kisses her hand, lingeringly.

Until we meet again then, Miss Pinchin.

ADELAIDE. Goodbye Mr Love.

She turns and walks upstage, remaining with her back to the audience.

GEORGE. Her hand was shaking. And damp. She was ripe for it. I watched her into the shop.

He does. They wave. He turns to audience.

Shame.

ADELAIDE. Everyone at work wanted to know what had happened to their fish. But I didn't say. Forgot to pick up the liver for tea and dad asked me what I was in such a daze about. After tea I tried to read but I kept forgetting to turn the pages. I felt dad watching me, I said my eyes were tired and went upstairs. I shut the door. Tried on the black velvet.

She looks at herself in an imaginary mirror. Doesn't like what she sees.

…had to wear the blue again. I hate the blue.

GEORGE. Next day I strolled through the cemetery, picked up a nice bunch of red roses. She was still wearing the blue. But she'd put some rouge on.

ADELAIDE. He'd bought some roses just for me. We went to the park and walked in the sunshine. Bought pies from a stall and listened to the band. He asked if I would take his arm as we walked.

She slips her arm through his.

GEORGE. She had little nervous fingers.

ADELAIDE. He laid his hand over mine.

GEORGE. They like that kind of thing.

ADELAIDE. We stopped by the pond and fed the last of our pies to the ducks. He seemed serious.

GEORGE. Miss Pinchin...

ADELAIDE. Yes Mr Love?

GEORGE. Miss Pinchin... I hardly slept last night.

ADELAIDE. Neither did I...

GEORGE. Thinking of you. Since the moment of our meeting, of our seeing one another, it is as if I've become possessed by your image.

ADELAIDE. Oh.

GEORGE. I have thought of nothing but you.

ADELAIDE. Oh.

GEORGE. Is it possible? To love so quickly?

ADELAIDE. Love?

GEORGE. Is it possible?

ADELAIDE. I don't know.

GEORGE. I think you do. I look into your eyes and I think you know as well as I. I think you knew the moment we saw each other through the window. I cannot tell you how much I ache to...

ADELAIDE. Yes?

GEORGE. Take you in my arms.

ADELAIDE. Yes.

GEORGE. Hold you to me.

ADELAIDE. Yes.

GEORGE. And say... Adelaide Pinchin, I want you for my wife.

ADELAIDE. Yes.

GEORGE. I cannot allow that to happen.

ADELAIDE. Oh...

GEORGE. You see – I have nothing to offer. No employment. No prospect of employment.

ADELAIDE. I thought you were with the diplomatic service.

GEORGE. I was invalided out. After service in Peking during the Boxer Rebellion. I took a bullet in the chest and it left me weak. All I have is a small allowance from an elderly aunt in Hastings. She has made it a stipulation of her kindness that I neither marry nor incur any extra debts throughout the remainder of her lifetime. One day of course the entire estate will come to me, but if I marry you now we will both be penniless.

They look at one another.

These two days have been such unlooked for pleasure to me. I have dared to allow myself such... visions of happiness...

ADELAIDE. Yes.

He turns away.

GEORGE. We must do the only proper thing and part company now. While we still can bear to do so.

ADELAIDE. No.

GEORGE. Please, my dear...

ADELAIDE. Perhaps you could talk to her, make her change her mind.

GEORGE. Impossible.

ADELAIDE. Or find a job.

GEORGE. My health is delicate.

ADELAIDE. I could keep working.

GEORGE. I have a little pride.

ADELAIDE. There must be something...

GEORGE. Nothing... nothing... unless...

ADELAIDE. What?

GEORGE. I couldn't ask you.

ADELAIDE. What?

GEORGE. You would have to risk everything. Your reputation, your family's displeasure, all for a man you hardly know...

ADELAIDE. What would I have to do?

GEORGE. Marry me now, as soon as possible in secret.

Her hesitation is fractional.

ADELAIDE. I'll do it.

GEORGE. You would have to be brave, resolute, certain beyond all question...

ADELAIDE. I'll do it.

GEORGE. When?

ADELAIDE. Tomorrow. Today if you want.

GEORGE. Adelaide. I suppose I may call you that?

ADELAIDE. Yes

GEORGE. Adelaide. My darling Adelaide.

They kiss.

We'd have to be very careful. Tell no one – absolutely no one.

ADELAIDE. What about mum and dad?

GEORGE. No one. Word gets about so easily – and they wouldn't understand.

ADELAIDE. But…

GEORGE. No one – until the time is right. Until then it must be our secret… yes?

ADELAIDE. Yes.

GEORGE. Promise and keep your promise.

ADELAIDE. I always keep my promises.

GEORGE. We're engaged then.

ADELAIDE. I'm so excited.

GEORGE. Go home and pack your bags.

ADELAIDE. I will.

GEORGE. And don't forget to bring a pretty nightie. A very pretty nightie. Something soft and silky.

His mouth skims hers.

For our wedding night.

Oh – and I suppose you'd better bring your bank book.

ADELAIDE. My bank book?

GEORGE. To have your account name changed.

ADELAIDE. Account name…

GEORGE. When we're married. You'd better bring your bank book so we can have your account name changed to Love, Mrs Love to-be.

ADELAIDE. Oh yes… I suppose so.

GEORGE. I'll get a special licence.

ADELAIDE. Oh yes…

GEORGE. We can be married by the end of the week.

ADELAIDE. Yes.

GEORGE. Goodbye my love, my sweet sweet love.

ADELAIDE. Oh George…

They face one another, moving slowly apart as they speak.

GEORGE. Picked up a ring in the pawnbroker's in Whitechapel High street. Brass. Bit green inside but good enough. Spent the next two days dodging the landlady and living on air.

ADELAIDE. I bought my wedding dress. Brown. I wanted a white one. There was a lovely white one… but I bought the brown. Sneaked it home without anyone seeing. I was that restless mum said I must be sickening for something and sent me to bed early. She brought up some hot milk. I nearly told her – mum I'm getting married tomorrow. I wanted to tell her. When she'd gone I packed my bag and hid it under my bed. Next day I was up before the dawn.

GEORGE. The bloody landlady was outside my door at eight o'clock, shouting about the police… Her little boy's trying to kick his way in. Time to be off. Slipped out the window and down a bit of tree growing outside. Legged it to Bell St. picking dead leaves out of my hair.

ADELAIDE. Put my dress on in the cloakroom at work then went outside to wait for him.

GEORGE. We walked to the registry office. She was wearing something brown and shiny.

ADELAIDE. He said I looked lovely.

He looks at her.

The lady who signed the book played the harmonium for us.

GEORGE. I kept gazing into her eyes so she wouldn't look too close at the ring.

ADELAIDE. I cried as he put it on my finger.

He does this.

GEORGE. Man and wife.

ADELAIDE. Man and wife.

They look into one another's eyes.

GEORGE. We walked to Paddington station. I was skint.
I'm afraid I have nothing smaller than a five pound note.

ADELAIDE. Oh.

GEORGE. I could break into it, but perhaps it might be simpler…

ADELAIDE. Oh yes.

She hands him the money.

GEORGE. Two singles to Weston Super Mare. First class.

The train whistles.

ADELAIDE. We sat by the window and watched the sights go by. I'd bought a bit of chocolate and I shared it out. He called it our wedding supper and kissed my cheek.

GEORGE. She fell asleep against my shoulder.

ADELAIDE. He felt strong and safe.

GEORGE. My arm went dead.

ADELAIDE. By the time we got to the seaside it was almost night.

They 'disembark' from the train, and while ADELAIDE *speaks the boarding house bedroom takes shape around them.*

We walked to the sea front. George said the fresh air would do us good.

GEORGE. We took a room in Glenfiddich boarding house.

ADELAIDE. Dark and dingy and smelling of fish.

She is inside, and registers her surroundings for the first time.

Back room.

GEORGE. Cheaper than a front.

ADELAIDE. Overlooking the back yard and the privy and the dustbins. But it didn't matter.

There is a small wind up gramophone in the corner. She sees it…

Oh look, George… we've got one like this at home. Let's see if it works.

She winds it up and does all the rest of it… The tinny notes of the merry widow waltz shudder out uncertainly.

Oh George I can't believe I'm here. I can't believe I'm here with you. I should be at home, washing up after tea or mending my stockings, or in my room, having a good read… I've done it haven't I? I've really done it. No going back now.

GEORGE. No going back.

He kisses her. He looks out at the audience over her shoulder.

Did you bring your bank book my darling?

ADELAIDE. What George dear?

GEORGE. You have brought it haven't you Adelaide?

ADELAIDE. Of course I have George, you told me to. Why?

GEORGE. Oh Adelaide I'm so ashamed.

ADELAIDE. Why?

GEORGE. I hardly know how to tell you why. How can I do this to you on our wedding night?

ADELAIDE. What George dear?

GEORGE. Adelaide – I am temporarily embarrassed.

ADELAIDE. What about George dear?

GEORGE. No. No I am temporarily financially embarrassed.

ADELAIDE. Oh.

GEORGE. My aunt – Eudora – from whom I receive my allowance has been taken ill before signing my monthly cheque.

ADELAIDE. Oh dear.

GEORGE. A small attack of gout – in the hands. I am in daily expectation of her recovery. But alas, I am at present...

He demonstrates a total want of financial resources.

ADELAIDE. Oh.

GEORGE. Yes... So I thought, since you had your bank book...

ADELAIDE. Of course George, what's mine is yours now.

GEORGE. Don't be angry with me Adelaide.

ADELAIDE. I'm not angry George. How much will we need?

GEORGE. I think it might as well be all of it Adelaide.

ADELAIDE. All of it?

GEORGE. If that's all right.

ADELAIDE. Of course. Of course you can have it all...it's never done me any good all the months I've had it anyway. We might as well spend it on being happy together.

GEORGE. Together. Forever. My darling wife...

They kiss.

It was time to perform my conjugal duty.

He is nuzzling into her... Throughout his next words she remains still, frozen in her own space.

Be a good husband and please my wife.

He draws his hands down her body.

Give her something to remember.

Slowly and sensuously...

A beacon to light the darkness of her declining years.

The only time in her life... The one and only time in her life...

He strokes her.

She got a bloody good shag.

He whispers almost against her ear.

Poor Mare.

He begins his routine. His recipe of seduction that has never failed him.

ADELAIDE. George… What are you doing?

GEORGE. Touching you Adelaide…

He continues his activity. She remains rigid, unresponsive, pained. After a while he pulls back, looks at her.

don't you like it?

ADELAIDE. I don't know…

GEORGE. You will, my darling, I'll make sure you will…

ADELAIDE. There's a little gas ring George. We could make a cup of tea… I've got some tea in my bag and a bit of sugar, and that penn'orth of milk I picked up at the station – we can have a nice cup of tea.

She pulls away. He looks out at us.

GEORGE. Shy… bless her.

ADELAIDE. There's two cups… Would you like the cracked one or the flowery one?

GEORGE. You choose.

ADELAIDE. My gran had cups like these.

GEORGE. Really?

While she speaks she picks up the kettle, shakes it, finds it full of water, puts it on the gas ring and lights the gas.

ADELAIDE. Yes. She had the whole set. Cups, saucers, tea plates, dinner plates, gravy boat and saucer… She even had the coffee cups and the coffee pot. Took her twelve years to collect them. She left them all to Aunt Lottie –

GEORGE. Really?

She goes to her bag and takes out the tea and other things. **GEORGE** *moves over to her and stands behind her.*

ADELAIDE. … and uncle Eugene sat on them while they were still in the box. Mum said it served them right because they were always acting flash and going to Venice and places and talking about it all the time afterwards.

With the tea things in her hands, turns around and finds herself looking into his eyes.

Have you been there?

GEORGE. Where?

ADELAIDE. Venice.

GEORGE. I don't remember.

ADELAIDE. You coudn't forget Venice George…

GEORGE. I been all over, they all look the same after a while.

ADELAIDE. But Venice! All those beautiful canals…

GEORGE. Oh yes, those… I remember… yes I've been there.

ADELAIDE. What was it like?

GEORGE. Very nice. Lots of canals.

ADELAIDE. And the Doge's Palace… and…

GEORGE. That too…

He takes both her arms, imprisoning them, obliging her to stay beside him. He draws her towards a chair, eases her down so that she is sitting on his knee. She perches there awkwardly.

… You've got nice hair Adelaide. Soft and shiny. How long is it when you let it down?

ADELAIDE. Not very…

GEORGE. Take it down Adelaide… please…

ADELAIDE. I will in a minute.

GEORGE. Take it down now Adelaide.

She begins to do so, leaving the tea things awkwardly in her lap, but even as her hands reach up the kettle shrieks into life. – She is off like a bullet to see to it. She makes tea while he slowly approaches her…

ADELAIDE. Do you like it strong or weak?

GEORGE. Either.

ADELAIDE. Do you take sugar?

GEORGE. No.

ADELAIDE. There you are then.

She gives him his tea.

GEORGE. Lovely…

He puts it down very slowly, without tasting it. He is smoothly confident. She stands motionless. Without speaking he begins to take down **ADELAIDE**'s *hair. She does not resist. He begins to comb it out with his fingers.*

ADELAIDE. Don't pull.

GEORGE. I won't.

He begins stroking her neck.

ADELAIDE. My mother will be wondering where I am. I've never been away from home before. But she'll be glad when she knows… Does your mother know about me?

GEORGE. No.

ADELAIDE. Will she mind?

GEORGE. I shouldn't think so… she's dead.

ADELAIDE. Oh dear.

He sees his opportunity.

GEORGE. Yes tragic, her punt capsized at Henley… she was dragged down by the voluminous folds of her white muslin dress.

ADELAIDE. Oh dear.

GEORGE. I still miss her. Ache to be held by her…

He nestles into her. She does not resist. He is certain he has vanquished.

Oh Adelaide…

He is guiding her down, onto the bed, manoeuvring her into position… He kisses her long and sensuously… When it is over.

ADELAIDE. We could play a little game of cards if you like George.

She is up, rummaging through her bag.

I've got a little pack in my bag. We could play rummy. I'm quite good at rummy… or beggar my neighbour. Or Newmarket. Or crib. Can you play crib? Men always know about cards. You better deal, I'm not very good at that.

She puts the cards on the bed beside him.

I take ages and the hands are never the same. Course it's all right with twenty-one. With twenty-one you only get two cards and I can manage that all right, but with whist I get in a real muddle. My dad's very good at whist, he almost always wins. He plays with his friends on Saturdays and sometimes me and mum make up the numbers. Farthing a point. I haven't got any coppers, have you? Doesn't matter, we can play for hair pins.

She discovers a little paper parcel while she is rummaging.

I've got a little bit of bread pudding in my bag too, in case we get hungry later. We could have it with a cup of tea, it's nice with a good hot cup of tea. All sugary on the top, like a bread pudding should be… Or there's a little shop on the corner, if it's still open we could get some nice biscuits. Digestives are nice with tea aren't they? I always like a digestive with tea…

GEORGE. Will you stop going on about the tea Adelaide?

ADELAIDE. Don't you like it? I should have thought. I should have brought some coffee.

GEORGE. I don't want any coffee.

ADELAIDE. I could nip out and see if that little shop on the corner's still open. They keep late hours don't they some little shops. I could nip out…

GEORGE. For God's sake Adelaide this is our bloody wedding night.

She looks at him in shock.

ADELAIDE. You swore.

GEORGE. No I didn't.

ADELAIDE. Yes you did. I hate it. My father always starts swearing on Saturday nights when he's played whist and had a few drinks. He always swears at mother for forgetting what's trumps. I hate men swearing.

GEORGE. I don't swear.

ADELAIDE. You just did.

GEORGE. I don't usually.

ADELAIDE. That's what Dad says.

GEORGE. Have you ever heard me swear before?

ADELAIDE. No, but I've only known you two days.

GEORGE. Look… I don't swear all right? And I don't want any bread pudding and I don't want to play rummy or crib or twenty-one. All right?

She is silent.

I love you Adelaide… you're my wife and I love you…

She looks at him.

So come here and let me hold you the way I want to.

She doesn't move.

ADELAIDE. I can't.

GEORGE. Of course you can. If you're shy we can turn down the light, make it cosy in the dark, there isn't that nice…

He turns down the lamp, all his movements practised, patient and gentle. He comes closer to her…

ADELAIDE. I'm sorry. I'm sorry George.

GEORGE. Adelaide…

He takes her in an embrace…

ADELAIDE. Don't. Don't… Just let me alone.

She pulls violently away from him.

GEORGE. Let you alone.

He registers the full impact of this.

Let you alone.

ADELAIDE. I don't want you to touch me… I'm sorry…

GEORGE. Is there something about me you find displeasing?

ADELAIDE. No.

GEORGE. I mean I have been told I am not without a certain grace and style, perhaps even handsomeness.

ADELAIDE. Yes.

GEORGE. I believe I know how to dress. I believe I know how to conduct myself as a gentleman.

ADELAIDE. It isn't you?

GEORGE. Then what is it?

ADELAIDE. Me.

GEORGE. What's the matter with you?

ADELAIDE. I'm the matter with me. I'm always the matter with me.

She stands in front of him. Expecting him to see what she means. He doesn't. He looks at her blankly.

Don't look at me.

GEORGE. What are you talking about?

ADELAIDE. Don't look at me. I hate what I look like.

GEORGE. Don't be silly…

He moves towards her, but her next word stops him.

ADELAIDE. No! He told me this would happen.

GEORGE. What?

ADELAIDE. Never get a husband. Look at you, who'd want that? You're just trying to be nice, I know you are, but I can't… If you see me you'll hate me…

GEORGE. Why?

ADELAIDE. Don't pretend please…

GEORGE. I'm not pretending

He isn't.

ADELAIDE. Fat cow he says…

GEORGE. Who says?

ADELAIDE. Never find a husband, never get rid of her… He knows. He's seen me. The only man who's ever seen me.

GEORGE. What are you talking about?

ADELAIDE. There was so much of me. I was all over the place, it was horrible.He just stood watching me with such a look on his face. I sat there in that little tin tub, a little puddle of water lapping around the edges of me, trying to gather everything up in my hands so he didn't have to see it.

GEORGE. What are you talking about?

ADELAIDE. I can't do it. I just can't. I shouldn't have come here.

GEORGE. Just a minute. Look, just a minute.

ADELAIDE. He told me… "God", he said, "pity the poor sod who has to unpack all that on his wedding night"…

Pause.

GEORGE. Who said that?…

ADELAIDE. I was fifteen in the bath in the back kitchen and he come in unexpectedly.

GEORGE. Your dad?

ADELAIDE. He put me on a diet. Clear soup and boiled fish. Sundays he'd have me stand in my singlet while he measured me. He'd keep a record of all the numbers week to week… I lost a lot of weight. And he was so pleased with me. "My good girl" he used to say, "my good girl's going to be a beauty". Hugging me all the time. I was so proud. I started cheating. I started buying things on the way home from work because I was so hungry. Cheese and apples and biscuits sometimes. Hide it in my room. Once he found them. He came down into the back kitchen and threw them on the table and just said one word – "why?" I tried to say but he just held up his hand as if to say there was no words to make it right. That's what I do: go to work in the back room with the other ugly ones, come home, sit in my room and eat and eat and eat, sometimes until I think I'll burst. Until I'm sick… Saturday nights when he's had a few drinks…

Silence.

Look at me. I'm wearing this on my wedding day…

She gestures at her brown outfit.

… all my nice clothes are too small.

GEORGE. Why are your nice clothes too small?

ADELAIDE. So they'll fit me when I lose weight.

He looks at her uncomprehendingly.

GEORGE. You're not fat.

ADELAIDE. Eighteen inch waist without corseting. That's what it should be. Look in the lady's journals. Is that an eighteen inch waist? Thick and fat. I've got everything planned for when I've lost weight. I've got this skirt in my wardrobe. Black velvet. When I've lost weight I'll wear it with this white silk blouse with little pearl buttons I keep wrapped in tissue paper… and then…

GEORGE. What?

ADELAIDE. Everything will be all right.

Pause.

GEORGE. Adelaide, listen. There's nothing wrong with you. You're not fat. Not a little bit. Look at you.

ADELAIDE. You're being nice.

GEORGE. No I'm not. Look at you.

ADELAIDE. Don't!

GEORGE. Oh come on. Look at yourself.

She won't.

Look at that sweet face hey? And those little hands. Clever little hands. And that little waist. You could be a Gibson girl.

ADELAIDE. I'm not a Gibson girl George.

GEORGE. Yes you are… Stop wearing brown, get yourself some white and pink, pink's your colour isn't it? Show your hair off a bit more… few pearls, on your ears, round your neck.

ADELAIDE. Don't…

GEORGE. You could go anywhere with the best of them. Straight you could. You could be up West in the best fashion emporium, look like a queen. Moment I first saw you in that window, I looked right at you and I thought…

For some reason his words fail him, he only; looks at her and she meets his eyes.

ADELAIDE. What did you think?

GEORGE. You were just what I was looking for.

There's a moment of silence.

ADELAIDE. Don't say that…

GEORGE. It's true.

ADELAIDE. If you want to go now…

GEORGE. What?

ADELAIDE. I won't complain… I won't come after you or anything if you want to go now…

GEORGE. Don't say that…

ADELAIDE. It might be best you know. You didn't expect all this, this isn't a wedding night.

GEORGE. It's our wedding night…

ADELAIDE. No, I can't…

GEORGE. All right… all right.

ADELAIDE. It wouldn't be that hard just to go back would it?

GEORGE. And then what? Stay there the rest of your life?

ADELAIDE. It's all right. I've got my room and my things. I've got my little job. Shopping with mum on Saturday morning. I know where I am.

GEORGE. And Saturday nights.

ADELAIDE. It's not that bad really…

GEORGE. Why would you say that?

ADELAIDE. It's where I belong

GEORGE. Listen Adelaide, here's a bit of advice. Take it if you've got any sense. Whatever you do, even if you walk out that door now, never go back there as long as you live.

ADELAIDE. I couldn't do that.

GEORGE. Yes you could. Take what you've got, and run…

ADELAIDE. Where?

GEORGE. Somewhere else.

ADELAIDE. It's my dad, my mum. I love them.

GEORGE. Oh yes and they love you.

ADELAIDE. Yes they do. Mum does.

GEORGE. Cos you go shopping on Saturdays?

ADELAIDE. We have nice times.

GEORGE. And what about the Saturday nights? Where is she then?

ADELAIDE. She gets headaches a lot Saturdays. She has to go to bed.

GEORGE. You're on your own.

ADELAIDE. It's not her fault.

GEORGE. Something I learned a long time ago, Adelaide – there's only two kinds of people in the world – the takers and the took.

ADELAIDE. That's not true.

GEORGE. In every happy home. There'll be the ones doing the taking and the ones being took. He's taking you. And she's letting him.

ADELAIDE. Don't be silly.

GEORGE. What would they do without you there? The world makes him feel small, there's you, waiting at home. Time he's finished with you he feels like a man again. If it wasn't you it'd be her wouldn't it? Or worse.

ADELAIDE. You don't know that.

GEORGE. So she gets a headache and let's him get on with it. Putting you in your place and keeping you there.

ADELAIDE. He's my father. What else should he do?

GEORGE. He could make you happy. It's not difficult making someone happy.

Pause.

I could make you happy.

Pause.

ADELAIDE. I should go home. I could go home now. Catch the next train. Tell a little story, no one would ever know.

GEORGE. Is that what you want?

ADELAIDE. I don't know.

GEORGE. They've got you haven't they? Her with her headaches and him... What is he? Some sort of genius? Some sort of god?

ADELAIDE. No... he's a clerk with the GWR.

GEORGE. Oh yes. And what's he like?

ADELAIDE. I don't know what you mean.

GEORGE. What's he like, I want to see him in here.

He gestures at his head.

ADELAIDE. Ordinary...

GEORGE. Is that all.

ADELAIDE. We're an ordinary family. It's what we are. Mum was in service. Dad's a clerk. Nothing wrong with that.

GEORGE. What does he look like?

ADELAIDE. Ordinary...

GEORGE. What's he wear?

ADELAIDE. He's got two black wool suits and a grey for Sundays.

GEORGE. Whiskers?

ADELAIDE. A little moustache. He reads the Daily Herald...his hair's going thin, but he combs it over so you can't see.

GEORGE. But it slips and you can.

ADELAIDE. Only sometimes.

They look at each other. They laugh.

Shouldn't laugh.

GEORGE. Why not?

ADELAIDE. He's my father.

Beat.

He puts macassar on to keep it in place. It takes him ages in front of the mirror arranging it. Trying to spread it all out wide enough... I suppose he's quite vain really... I never thought of that before. He's got these silver backed brushes and he keeps them polished up all the time. The only things he ever cleans in the whole house. His hair brushes and the little silver dish he keeps his pipe in...

GEORGE. When he's sitting there, do you ever want to tell him – I can see your bald patch.

ADELAIDE. It's all coming undone at the back.

GEORGE. But you don't.

ADELAIDE. It wouldn't do any good.

GEORGE. Wouldn't it?

She shakes her head wordlessly.

You know what he is don't you?

She doesn't answer.

How kids at school catch spiders and things, mess around with them instead of doing sums. You know the sort of thing… Mostly we'd just play with them a bit and let them go. But there's always one isn't there. Always one… who keeps his spider in his empty ink well. All day. And every so often he takes it out and very carefully, very slowly pulls one of its legs off. Just one. Just one at a time. Sometimes he works joint by joint, bit by little bit. Making it last as long as he can… Nipping and nipping… They never grow out of it that sort. Bit by bit, joint by joint, pulling you apart…

He becomes the father – his voice hectoring, wheedling, insinuating.

You're no use Adelaide. Look at you. Who'd love you but me? Where'd you be without your dear old dad? And Saturday nights hey? Saturday nights when he's had the whiskies. After his pals have all gone home and you mum's got her headache and there's no one to see.

ADELAIDE. No.

GEORGE. Pushing up to you. Is that it? Squeezing and nipping. Who'd love you but me Adelaide. Who'd put up with you but me Adelaide? So be a nice good girl, hey, and know your place…

Silence for as long as it will hold.

ADELAIDE. How do you know?

GEORGE. I've got psychic powers.

ADELAIDE. Really?

GEORGE. No, not really.

ADELAIDE. He doesn't mean it.

GEORGE. Don't say it.

ADELAIDE. It's all right really. I don't mind really… he can't help it.

GEORGE. What does it take? What does it take for a woman like you? Look at yourself. You've got fifty quid and a brooch worth twice as much again, you could have been out there. Free. But oh no. You have to bury yourself alive, with a thing like that…

He goes to her and takes her hands. She makes an effort to pull away. Over the next six lines they speak almost in unison.

ADELAIDE. No…

GEORGE. … There's nothing wrong with you. Except him. He's poison. Pouring himself into you. Just get out. And don't ever go back, Not for anything. Not on his dying day. He'll say he loves you, he'll say what can he do without you –

ADELAIDE. You don't know –

GEORGE. He'll sit there looking pathetic, trying to worm his way into you, trying to make you feel sorry for him –

ADELAIDE. Stop it –

GEORGE. But you've got to rip all that out of yourself, rip it out by the roots because it's a con trick, the biggest con in the world.

ADELAIDE. No.

GEORGE. It just wraps round you, chokes you alive. You have to rip it out. You don't listen to him. Walk out and shut the door. And you're free. Nothing can stop you once you're out that door. You're flying. You're laughing. And no one can touch you. Don't waste your tears on him or anyone. Miserable old bastard. The only chance you've got is to get away. Now. I'm telling you get away now while you still can. And swear to yourself that no one – no one – is ever going to twist you up like that again.

ADELAIDE. Stop shouting.

GEORGE. I'm not shouting, I don't shout… I'm just sick of listening to this song…

He stops abruptly, biting back his last words. His voice has reached a climax of intensity. **ADELAIDE** *is staring at him.*

ADELAIDE. What?

GEORGE. Nothing… just… nothing

He breaks away from her.

Silence.

ADELAIDE. What should I do?

GEORGE. Don't go back there.

ADELAIDE. What about mum…?

GEORGE. She'll have to choose, you or him.

ADELAIDE. I can't ask her…

GEORGE. Yes you can.

ADELAIDE. No, I can't… There's good in everyone.

GEORGE. No there isn't.

ADELAIDE. There's good in everyone, but you've got to look for it sometimes. That's what Rose says.

GEORGE. Who's Rose?

ADELAIDE. Girl I work with in the back room. She says happiness is finding the good in what you've got.

GEORGE. And what's she got?…

ADELAIDE. Not much. Funny teeth and a sister with polio. But she sings while she's working.

She sings a small snatch of tune.

I'LL BE YOUR SWEETHEART
IF YOU WILL BE MINE

Silence.

I know you're the best thing that ever happened to me. Don't think I don't.

GEORGE. You don't have to be grateful.

ADELAIDE. I am.

GEORGE. No. Be proud.

ADELAIDE. Proud?

GEORGE. Hold your head up… come on. You're a lovely woman.

ADELAIDE. Don't say that.

GEORGE. You're a lovely woman. I'm telling you what I see now as I'm looking at you. A lovely woman. With pretty hair and nice hands, and a sweet face. A clever woman who can make her own way in the world and owe nothing to anyone. Starting now.

He takes her hands.

ADELAIDE. It can't be that easy.

GEORGE. It can if you want it to be. Do you want it to be?

ADELAIDE. Yes.

GEORGE. Then it is. Just stop believing him and start believing me.

ADELAIDE. I want to.

GEORGE. Then do it. Say George, I believe you.

ADELAIDE. George…

GEORGE. I believe you…

ADELAIDE. I believe you.

GEORGE. And hold your head up.

> *She does.*

> Now come on… look at yourself in the mirror…

> *He guides her to the glass.*

ADELAIDE. No. I hate mirrors.

GEORGE. No you don't. Come and look in the mirror.

> *He turns her head towards her reflection.*

> See? What do you see?

ADELAIDE. Me. Just me.

GEORGE. No, that's Mrs Love. Mrs Love. With pretty hair, see? And nice hands… and soft skin… see? See?

> *She looks.*

ADELAIDE. Yes.

GEORGE. See her?

ADELAIDE. Yes.

GEORGE. So do I… and she's happy isn't she?

> *He is cradling her as they both look.*

ADELAIDE. Yes.

GEORGE. Remember that. You don't need him or anyone else to make you something.

ADELAIDE. I need you. Because I love you, Mr Love.

> *They look at one another for as long as it will hold. This is not sexual tension, but something else.*

GEORGE. Adelaide…

ADELAIDE. Yes?

> *Pause, as if he hardly knows what he might be about to say…*

GEORGE. Have you got those cards?

ADELAIDE. Of course I have.

GEORGE. And enough hair pins?

ADELAIDE. Hundreds.

GEORGE. Get them out then why don't you? We can have a game of twenty-one.

ADELAIDE. Don't you mind?

GEORGE. I don't mind.

ADELAIDE. It isn't that I don't want...

He silences her by touching her lips.

GEORGE. I can wait... there's plenty of time.

Pause.

Get the cards hey?

ADELAIDE. All right George.

GEORGE. I could show you Russian Twenty-one. As taught me by Grand Duke Michael himself.

ADELAIDE. That sounds nice.

GEORGE. We should have vodka and caviar as an accompaniment, but failing that I suppose there'd be nothing wrong with a cup of tea.

ADELAIDE. I suppose not.

She hesitates.

And there's the bread pudding if we get hungry.

GEORGE. It sounds lovely...

She is joyous.

ADELAIDE. All right then George. A nice game of Russian twenty-one and a good hot cup of tea to warm us both up, how about that?

GEORGE. How about it?

ADELAIDE. Thank you.

GEORGE. I said don't thank me.

ADELAIDE. Be proud.

She turns away and walks up stage. Picks up the kettle to take it out and fill it...

GEORGE. I bet I beat you rotten.

ADELAIDE. It doesn't matter... I don't mind losing...

She disappears into shadows. He stands alone. He can be heard softly humming the song she sang earlier. He sees his own face in the mirror and looks into his own eyes as the lights dim to black.

End of Act One

ACT TWO

Half light, like dawn or early morning. **ADELAIDE** *is lying on the bed.* **GEORGE** *is sitting on a chair, watching the sleeping woman. There is a sense that he may have been there for many hours, watching. He wears only shirt, trousers and waistcoat. Jacket and tie discarded. As the light increases he turns to the audience.*

GEORGE. Had the timetable all worked out. Train to Bristol at a quarter to eleven. I was going to be on that. With fifty quid in my pocket.

He stops, looking down at her.

Snoring. Mouth open. Hair all over the place.

He looks at her a moment before touching her. She wakes with a grunt and a start.

ADELAIDE. All right… it's all right now… I forgot where I was for a minute.

GEORGE. I thought I'd scared you.

ADELAIDE. No. I thought I was at home. What time is it?

GEORGE. Half-past nine.

ADELAIDE. Golly. You should have woken me.

GEORGE. You needed your sleep. We were playing cards till half past five.

ADELAIDE. So we were.

GEORGE. I got the hair pins to prove it.

ADELAIDE. They won't be much use to you.

GEORGE. You'll have to win them back then.

ADELAIDE. I will if we play Rummy. I'm good at Rummy.

GEORGE. Rummy's a kid's game. I'll teach you Brag.

ADELAIDE. I'll never learn.

GEORGE. Yes you will, I'm a good teacher. Best be getting up.

They look at one another.

ADELAIDE. I enjoyed myself ever such a lot. Thank you – for everything.

GEORGE. Don't thank me. You'd better be getting up.

ADELAIDE. Why?

GEORGE. There's things to do. You'll have to telegraph your parents about where you are…

ADELAIDE. Oh yes, I'd forgotten about that. They'll be that worried. I should have done it last night.

She gets up. She puts on her hat. He puts on his bowler.

We strolled along the front. looking out at the sea, and the people on the sand. And the sun on the water. My arm in his.

GEORGE. We strolled to the bank.

ADELAIDE. I informed them of my change of name… and withdrew the money.

She picks the money up from the table while he watches her.

Fifty-one pounds five shillings and eightpence three farthing.

She begins to put the money away in her little bag.

Are you all right George?

GEORGE. Why do you ask?

ADELAIDE. You look a bit… funny.

GEORGE. Do I? Oh.

ADELAIDE. I was thinking, George, would you mind looking after this for me?

She looks up at him.

It's much safer in an inside pocket isn't it?

GEORGE. I suppose it is.

ADELAIDE. And there's such a lot of it. I'd be frightened all the time of losing it. If you're sure you don't mind.

He takes it from her.

GEORGE. Of course not.

He puts it away in his pocket.

ADELAIDE. Is there something wrong George?

GEORGE. Just a touch of headache dear. I think I might go and lie down.

ADELAIDE. You do look pale.

GEORGE. Yes. I'll go back to the room and lie down.

ADELAIDE. I'll come with you.

GEORGE. No… no I'll be fine on my own, you see the sights. Send your telegram. I'll be waiting when you get back.

ADELAIDE. All right.

GEORGE. Here.

He gives her the five shillings etc.

Buy yourself something nice in the shops and come back and show me.

ADELAIDE. But I don't know where to go, I've never been here before…

GEORGE. You'll find your way… and I'll be waiting…

He kisses her hand.

Don't be too long.

He steps away from her backwards, slowly releasing her hand. She watches him.

Take care my darling…

ADELAIDE. I will.

Slowly he moves away.

GEORGE. I kept to a walk, a slow walk until I was round the corner, and then… I was away. I was free. Running. Running free. Down the street. Back to the boarding house. Up to the room. Clock on the landing said ten past ten. Just enough time. Got my bag and threw in my clothes. Searched through hers, took what there was worth taking, no more than a fiver's worth. Her jacket was lying on the chair, real silk, I was going to have that…

He stops. Out of breath.

It smelt of her.

He looks about.

The room smelt of her. English Rose. Little bottle of English Rose scent on the dressing table.

He goes to it, picks it up, looks at it, momentarily haunted. He puts the bottle down, uncertain, but then his eye focuses on something else.

And next to it her brooch. Auntie Myra's brooch.

He picks it up, looking at it. He is centred again.

Some people just shouldn't be let out on their own...

He pockets it.

ADELAIDE. Sent my telegram. Dear mum safe and well and married to Mr Love stop Contact care of Glenfiddich boarding house, Weston Super Mare stop see you soon stop love from Mrs Love.

GEORGE. I was out and down into the street, walking towards the station, thinking about the money and what I'd do with it. The things I'd do with it.

ADELAIDE. I saw something in the window of a little shop on the corner. A long chemise all soft and shiny. I looked at it for ever such a long time...

GEORGE. The sun was shining down on my face. Hot. Fished in my pocket for my handkerchief.

He does. He draws it out. The brooch is entangled and falls to the floor. Slowly he picks it up.

One of the stupid little bows was knocked crooked. I straightened it.

He does, looking at it.

Stupid little bows. Ugly little thing. I thought about her coming back and me long gone with the money and Auntie Myra's precious brooch... Knowing herself for what she was, knowing... I wanted to laugh...

He looks at it.

I turned round. I turned round. And walked – walked back to the boarding house.

ADELAIDE. Then I went in and bought it. Without even trying it on. I went in. And bought it. And went back to the boarding house, hurrying back, pushing through the people...

GEORGE. up the stairs, open the door.

He does. He looks at the brooch a moment. He tosses it down on to the dressing table. It seems to wake him from a kind of trance.

ADELAIDE. I missed the turning and had to go back.

GEORGE. Good riddance to you, you old bag.

ADELAIDE. A church clock struck half-past ten.

GEORGE. Fifteen minutes to get the train and get out.

He grabs up his bag.

ADELAIDE. Up the stairs.

GEORGE. I had my hand on the door.

ADELAIDE. Open the door…

They confront one another. They look at one another for as long as it will hold.

What are you doing George? Are you better? You look better.

Silence. She comes into the room, puts down her shopping.

I did what you said George. I bought something nice.

She takes the chemise from her bag and holds it against her. It's a pale soft pink.

Took most of the five bob. It's a nightie. Crepe de chine. I never had a pretty nightie before. Hope it fits.

She looks at **GEORGE** *for a response. There is none.*

The lady in the shop said I could have my money back if it didn't fit, but I think it will… I thought I could wear it… tonight.

She looks for a sign of approbation.

If you'd like me to.

Pause.

Is everything all right George?

GEORGE. Why do you ask?

ADELAIDE. You're acting funny…

GEORGE. It's the headache. I think I need a powder. You couldn't pop out to the Chemist's could you and…

ADELAIDE. I've got a headache powder in my bag George, shall I mix it for you?

GEORGE. Yes please.

She does.

I think I might need a breath of air, perhaps I'll have a stroll while it's mixing. Go down to the sea.

ADELAIDE. Oh lovely, I'll come with you. We haven't been on the beach yet.

GEORGE. Come to think of it I believe the tide's in.

ADELAIDE. Oh.

GEORGE. I'll just pop out and see.

ADELAIDE. Better wait until your headache's gone.

She hands the stuff to him. He drinks it.

I had a thought while I was out George – we never counted those bank notes after we got them…

GEORGE. Oh?

ADELAIDE. Do you think we should – just to make sure?

GEORGE. I'll do it later…

ADELAIDE. I thought I might have a bath later. If we could get some hot water. I could do with it after sleeping in these. And I couldn't put this on all dirty. I thought I could have a bath… and then put this on…

GEORGE. Why wait till later?

ADELAIDE. What?

GEORGE. You could have one now.

ADELAIDE. Now?

GEORGE. I'll go and order the water…

ADELAIDE. But it's only morning.

GEORGE. That doesn't have to worry us. I want to see you in this.

ADELAIDE. Really?

GEORGE. Really.

ADELAIDE. I might not look right.

GEORGE. You will.

Beat.

I'll order your bath, and then you can show me what you look like in that.

She has seen something.

ADELAIDE. What have you been doing with your bag George?

GEORGE. … I was just… packing. Ready for tomorrow.

ADELAIDE. Tomorrow?

GEORGE. Yes. I thought we could go on to somewhere nicer. Now we have your… the… our money. Paris or Brussels… or Venice.

ADELAIDE. Venice?

GEORGE. Why not? All those beautiful canals…

ADELAIDE. Oh George! St. Mark's Square. The Grand Canal. I can go in a gondola.

GEORGE. Of course you can.

ADELAIDE. If you're with me.

GEORGE. I'll order your bath.

ADELAIDE. All right. A nice big deep bath. Two cans of hot and a big white towel.

GEORGE. A nice deep bath with two cans of hot and a big white towel coming up my precious…

ADELAIDE. And while I'm waiting I could count the money.

GEORGE. I suppose you could…

He delivers the money back into her care…

Don't know how long it took for the water to boil. Felt like twenty years. I was thinking… Soon as she's in the bath I'm away. Sod the bag, I can get another bag, just get out with the money… Take the next train to anywhere, then another to somewhere else. Get shot of her, get bloody shot…

While he speaks **ADELAIDE** *flicks through the money and puts it aside. She picks up his misplaced hat. She puts it back where it belongs. She puts her hand to her throat, missing her brooch. She looks in the place she last put it. The brooch is not there. She looks about the room, increasingly alarmed. She can't find it. She sees her jacket missing from the chair… She sits down on the bed and looks at the bag…*

Helped the landlady drag the bath up two flights of stairs. Took twelve more trips to fetch the bleeding water.

She looks at his bag. She looks at him.

Nice and hot, just right. Nice towel too. Big and soft. For when you get out… So why don't you get in? What are you doing, eh? Gazing into space.

ADELAIDE. I don't know.

GEORGE. Still with your coat on. You need looking after you do.

ADELAIDE. Do I George?

GEORGE. Coat off. Come on… sit on the bed and I'll undo your boots.

ADELAIDE. No, I can do it.

He kneels before her, unbuttoning her boots.

GEORGE. I've got to get you ready for the bath. And while you're soaking I'll nip out.

ADELAIDE. Nip out?

GEORGE. Just for a moment. To that little shop on the corner, fetch us a bottle of something sparkly. Hey? something special and expensive…

ADELAIDE. All right George…

GEORGE. And we'll drink it while you're getting dry in front of the fire… hey?

ADELAIDE. Have you seen my brooch George?

He looks at her.

I can't find it. I've looked everywhere for it.

GEORGE. No. I expect it'll turn up.

ADELAIDE. I'm frightened I've lost it somewhere… Auntie Myra's brooch…

GEORGE. You haven't lost it, it's… in the room somewhere. I'll have a look for it when I get back. Now hop in while it's nice and hot.

ADELAIDE. I was thinking what if someone stole it, while I was out…

GEORGE. Of course no one's stolen it.

ADELAIDE. You can't be sure.

GEORGE. No one's stolen it, Adelaide… I'll have a look for it when I get back.

He picks up the money, is reaching for his hat.

ADELAIDE. All right George.

GEORGE. I'll be back in a tick…

He moves to the door.

ADELAIDE. Don't forget your bag George.

Silence.

They look at one another.

You have to stop pretending now.

GEORGE. Pretending?

ADELAIDE. Yes dear…

GEORGE. I don't know what you're talking about.

ADELAIDE. I'm talking about pretending George. I'm talking about lying. I'm talking about you lying to me.

GEORGE. Me? I never lied to a soul… I wouldn't know how. I was known for it in the diplomatic service, it got me into more scrapes than anything else. If it hadn't been for influence in high places I would have been in serious trouble once or twice... I remember in Paris...

ADELAIDE. What's the French for 'I love you', George?

He says nothing.

What's the French for 'I've never lied to a soul'? Please George, one word if you can...

He says nothing.

You were never in the diplomatic service. You weren't ever in Khartoum, nor Calcutta neither. Or Venice. You weren't shot in Peking during the boxer rebellion. And you haven't got a Fabergé egg. It was all lies. All of it lies... You told me a lot of lies so you could take all my money and never come back.

GEORGE. No Adelaide... Oh God yes. Yes. I did say some things that weren't quite true. Yes. I was a fool. I made up some things – but only to impress you. I made myself sound the way I wanted to be – for you. No. I don't speak French. No I haven't got a Fabergé egg. I'm an ex-soldier, that's all, just a junior officer, wounded in the Boer War, living off an army pension. I didn't think that would impress you. And I wanted to impress you so much – because I fell in love with you the moment I saw you. But you can't think I was going to... you mustn't think...

She speaks over him.

ADELAIDE. Have you got my clothes in there?

She indicates his bag.

GEORGE. What?

ADELAIDE. Is that where my wedding jacket is? How much would that have fetched you? And my brooch?

Beat.

Were you going to take that too? Were you going to take my brooch when you knew what it meant to me?

GEORGE. No I wasn't going to take your brooch.

ADELAIDE. I don't believe you.

GEORGE. I wasn't going to take your brooch. I wasn't going to take your precious brooch.

He finds it wherever it is and hurls it at her feet.

See...? See?

She bends down to retrieve it.

ADELAIDE. I couldn't find it.

GEORGE. Well maybe you should have looked.

She remains, looking at the brooch in her hand, thinking...

ADELAIDE. I'm sorry.

GEORGE. You're tired. It's been a lot of strain on you. You're getting nervy, imagining things.

ADELAIDE. Do you think so?

GEORGE. I know so. No sleep. A lot of excitement. What do you expect? Me running off and leaving you. What next hey?

ADELAIDE. I suppose we're not really married are we? I suppose you'd make sure of that. I've read about that sort of thing in the papers. I suppose you give a false name and that makes it all illegal… I suppose you've done it hundreds of times before. You must be clever to get away with it so much.

GEORGE. Look, I told you…

ADELAIDE. What's it feel like? I suppose you feel… clever. I can picture it. Clever and strong and free. Moving on, money in your pocket, nothing can touch you. And making people love you… it must be lovely to make people love you…

Despite himself he's flattered.

You have got a lovely smile. Only you're not smiling now.

GEORGE. What do you expect… my own wife…

ADELAIDE. I've got to get back. I'm missing a day's work. They dock you more than a day's pay if you don't have a sick note. I haven't got a sick note. They'll all be up in arms. There's the lavender toque coming in for finishing Saturday, for a wedding. Mrs Pear will send round to our house… And I sent that telegram… They've got it by now. Love from Mrs Love.

She looks at the nightie, picks it up.

Have you got a real wife somewhere else?

GEORGE. What is this?

ADELAIDE. Have you?

GEORGE. No.

ADELAIDE. Are you sure?

GEORGE. Yes.

ADELAIDE. I don't want to go back.

A silence.

As I see it. There's two things we can do. We can go our separate ways now. You can pick up your bag and leave… Or…

GEORGE. Or?

ADELAIDE. Stay with me. Stay married to me.

Beat.

I know what you're thinking, but just listen for a minute. If you stopped with me at least you wouldn't have to worry about being found out all the time. Stands to reason if you keep doing this sooner or later you'll get caught and it would be off to prison. And you're not getting any younger. I mean you can't keep doing this forever. It must take it out of you. Haven't you ever thought how nice it'd be to have a cosy home to come back to? Somewhere warm and safe? You'd have a roof over your head. I keep a clean house. Crisp sheets, well ironed and pressed with lavender. Nice warm fire in the winter. And I'm a good cook. You wouldn't want for anything.

GEORGE. You're going to provide for me?

ADELAIDE. Why not?

He laughs.

I've got fifty pounds. We could use it – together.

GEORGE. That wouldn't last long darling.

ADELAIDE. Well, we could get more… We could start up a business.

GEORGE. What sort of business?

ADELAIDE. A milliners.

GEORGE. A hat shop?

ADELAIDE. Yes.

GEORGE. You and me open a hat shop.

ADELAIDE. Why not? I've got the money, and you've got…everything else. We'd be ever such a good team. I could do the making and you could do the selling.

GEORGE. I didn't know I'd married an entrepreneur. My little wife is quite a surprise. Well well well…

ADELAIDE. What do you think?

GEORGE. I think I love you all the more.

ADELAIDE. What do you think?

GEORGE. You haven't even got a premises.

ADELAIDE. No but I know where it should be.

GEORGE. Yes?

ADELAIDE. A little corner place on the Cromwell Road. With a lantern outside and pretty windows.

GEORGE. That's just a little dream.

ADELAIDE. No. It's been vacant seven weeks this Monday. I keep walking past just to see.

GEORGE. You what?

ADELAIDE. It used to be a little dress shop. And it did well. Right sort of clientele. Middle class but not rich enough to shop in Mayfair.

GEORGE. You have thought about this haven't you.

ADELAIDE. I know just how we'd do the place up too…

GEORGE. Walking past every day on your way to work.

ADELAIDE. … All in green and gold. With red velvet chairs. And gold mirrors. And potted palms. And a big sign outside in fancy writing… Love's Milliners. Of Refinement and Quality… And there I'd be.

GEORGE. Picturing yourself…

ADELAIDE. With my own little office. Like Mrs Pear's only better. And I'd wear my white silk blouse and black velvet skirt.

GEORGE. You've got it all planned. So – how come you're not there already? Comfy in your little shop on the Cromwell Road?

She doesn't answer.

You've got your money.

She doesn't answer.

You were too afraid.

ADELAIDE. …We'd have a few of the best girls to do the everyday work.

And there you'd be in a black silk morning coat with a red carnation in your buttonhole. Mr Love. A gentleman of business.

Pause.

I've always been too afraid.

Pause.

GEORGE. How do you know they'd come to you?

ADELAIDE. Because I'm good. I'm very good George. I've got good hands. And I've got style. Everything I make has got that bit of style in it. Look…

She fetches her wedding hat.

I made this. See the ruching. See? Not one milliner in a hundred can better that. I'm good George. I'm too good for where I am. I've always been too good for where I am. And I've got ideas. I'm bursting with ideas. I could match anything the best fashion house in the world can do. I've just always been too afraid…

GEORGE. What sort of money are we talking about?

ADELAIDE. Enough.

GEORGE. What's enough?

ADELAIDE. More than you've got now anyway. And regular. A nice regular income.

GEORGE. Who has title of the shop?

ADELAIDE. We both do.

GEORGE. And the profits?

ADELAIDE. Equal shares.

GEORGE. Whose game is this?

ADELAIDE. What do you think?

Silence for as long as it will hold… He goes to his suitcase. Opens it. Takes out a reasonably full half bottle of whisky.

GEORGE. How about a drink? Hey? Drop of whisky. Found this downstairs last night.

ADELAIDE. You just took it?

GEORGE. No one seemed to want it.

He pours some into a cup.

Not the best, but good enough.

ADELAIDE. What do you think?

GEORGE. Why not? Why not, hey? Black morning coat and a red carnation – walking the floor. Course we'd have to do it right.

ADELAIDE. I know that.

GEORGE. Know what we wanted and go for it. No messing.

ADELAIDE. I thought we'd make up a little leaflet and send it out to all the professional people and the prosperous trades people…

GEORGE. Trades people. Forget that. We don't want trades people. Nor crummy little accountants' wives neither…

ADELAIDE. But…

GEORGE. That's just dragging along… thing is to think grand.

ADELAIDE. But…

Be smart. Be exclusive. You can get away with anything if you're exclusive. Think of the most you can expect someone to pay for something and double it. They'll pay. You don't believe me? I'll show you. Give me six months and I'll show you. I could get you the best return on fifty pounds anyone's ever seen…

He is smooth…

To be honest with you Lady Someone you are the only customer we have with enough natural good taste to know that the fifty guinea toque is the only one to wear if one wants to be coquettish without descending into mere…vulgarity. Before you know it you're making hats for Ascot. The cream of society waiting to be wooed and stroked and parted from their money.

And I'd stroke them and woo them…

I wouldn't let you tell them lies…

GEORGE. Who's talking about lies? Just slip them a little dream. And make them pay a fair price for it. Quid pro quo.

He holds up his cup.

To a new beginning.

ADELAIDE. Really?

GEORGE. To your making. And my selling. To a good team. To us.

ADELAIDE. Really?

GEORGE. Really…

ADELAIDE. You wouldn't be sorry.

GEORGE. Do you think I don't know that?

He laughs.

Love's Milliners.

He writes it up in his imagination.

That's all right isn't it? To celebrating the first profits with a beef supper and a bottle of burgundy. To this time next year in our new house – in Mayfair…

ADELAIDE. Mayfair?

GEORGE. Mayfair.

She makes an almost wordless interjection.

Housemaid, parlourmaid, butler and valet. Carriage and pair. We could take the town.... And then – Paris...

ADELAIDE. Paris?

GEORGE. Why not? Just see yourself. Finest Paris clothes. Hair just so. You'd look like a Gibson Girl. And the nights at the Opera. And the Soirées. Waltzing in a gold and silver ball room. You in a sleeveless ball gown, me in white tie and tails... Champagne every day. Quails eggs for breakfast...

He goes to the gramophone and winds it up.

May I have the pleasure of this dance Mrs Love? A little dance. One dance. No harm in dancing with your husband...

He takes her arms and swings her about.

ADELAIDE. If we caught an early train we could talk to the agent about the lease...

GEORGE. What's the hurry? We've got the room till two o'clock. You could have your bath, show me your new nightie.

ADELAIDE. And what would you do?

GEORGE. Whatever you wanted me to.

He swings her about in the dance.

You just have to tell me what you want and it's yours.

ADELAIDE. I want to be happy...

GEORGE. That's easy. Shut your eyes... go on shut your eyes. You're in your Paris Salon. Wearing silk and eating Pâté de Foie Gras. Feel it on your lips... the food of kings...

ADELAIDE. I can't, I've never tasted it...

GEORGE. Then imagine it...

ADELAIDE. I don't like it.

GEORGE. Of course you do.

ADELAIDE. It's too rich, it'll make me sick...

GEORGE. You'll get used to it.

ADELAIDE. I'll have the little beef dinner instead.

GEORGE. It's off the menu.

ADELAIDE. I can have what I want, that's what you said.

GEORGE. You can't have little beef dinners in Paris.

ADELAIDE. Then we'll have to stay here. Won't we?

GEORGE. Whatever you say.

He refils his cup.

ADELAIDE. Here… Last night. Playing cards for hair pins till it was nearly morning. Sharing the bread pudding. I was happy then. Happier than I've ever been. Were you?

He says nothing.

GEORGE. Beef then. Here's to you, dear old boiled beef. You and me. And a little busy hat shop on the Cromwell Road. You've got your office. And a nice little house. You and me on Margate sand, eating winkles with a pin out of a paper bag, sharing the pin for a laugh. You in a damp bathing hat dripping everywhere. Me in a summer blazer smelling of mothballs. Bringing half the beach home in our shoes and stopping on the way for fish and chips. You and me. Smiling at one another over the accounts. You and me either side of the fire on rainy Sundays. Me with the paper, you with your knitting. There's a cat somewhere. And a canary in a little cage. You and me making hats for tradesmen's wives. Cooking meals and eating them and going places and coming back. You and me one on top of the other in some bloody council cemetery, together forever and ever.

ADELAIDE. That's the way it is for everyone…

GEORGE. Not for me.

ADELAIDE. Why didn't you take my brooch?

GEORGE. What?

ADELAIDE. You said it was worth a lot of money. You took everything else. Why didn't you take it?

Pause.

I thought perhaps it was because you knew what it meant to me. Because you cared. Just a bit. Just a little bit… did you?

GEORGE. You're my wife Adelaide, of course I care about you.

ADELAIDE. Tell the truth.

GEORGE. My name's George Love. I was born in Venice while my parents were stationed over there with the embassy, my first memory was floating down the beautiful canals in a gondola while my mother wore her black velvet skirt and everything was all right…

ADELAIDE. Were you happy?

GEORGE. Deliriously, all those canals, who wouldn't be?

ADELAIDE. Last night. Here with me… Drinking tea and eating bread pudding.

GEORGE. Bread pudding – a favourite with General Gordon as I remember. Drowned at the siege of Ladysmith when his punt capsized, dragged down by the voluminous folds of his white muslin…

ADELAIDE. Stop it.

GEORGE. I don't play other people's games. And I won't be kept by my wife. The very thought Adelaide. We'll live off my allowance until Auntie Myra's no longer with us.

ADELAIDE. You haven't got an Auntie Myra .

GEORGE. I didn't say Myra I said… Beatrice.

ADELAIDE. It was Eudora yesterday.

He puts his drink down and makes for his jacket.

GEORGE. Oh yes of course Eudora. Beatrice was the other one with the diamond mine in California and the priceless collection of Siamese finger painting. She'd send me chocolate every Christmas wrapped in real gold leaf and ran off to Tibet with a man who played the spoons. I'm going out for a little walk while you clear your head, dear. When I come back we can pack and catch the boat train.

ADELAIDE. You're frightened aren't you? You're just running away frightened. Go then. I won't come after you, I won't fetch the police, but you have to tell me you're not coming back. Look in my face and tell me you're going to get on the train and ride away and never come back…

GEORGE. I'm…

He looks at her.

Going for a walk.

ADELAIDE. Then I'll come with you, we can see if the tide's in.

GEORGE. Your bath will get cold

ADELAIDE. It doesn't matter I'll have one on the boat train tonight.

GEORGE. They don't have baths on the boat train.

ADELAIDE. I'll have one in the hotel then when we get to France.

GEORGE. It's cold.

ADELAIDE. I like the cold.

GEORGE. It's raining.

ADELAIDE. I've got an umbrella.

GEORGE. What do you want?

ADELAIDE. You know.

GEORGE. All right. All right. I'm a crook. I go around the country marrying women and stealing everything they've got. I've been doing it since I was eighteen years old – well it's better than working isn't it? – and that's what I was going to do to you. I should have been on the train now, halfway to Bristol. Only last night… last night… last night I looked at you, here in this room. And I knew I loved you. Is that what you want me to say?

ADELAIDE. Only if it's true. Is it true?

Pause, he looks at her…

GEORGE. Yes. It's all true. I love you. And your tea. And your hair pins. And your little hands. And your sweet face. I love you. More preciously and tenderly than I have ever loved anything. I want to hold you in my arms and keep you warm and safe and make you smile. I ache when I look at you. When you look at me I feel stripped and weak and helpless and I know you could destroy me with a word. I'm weak with love for you. I want to go down on my knees and kiss the hem of your gown. I want to worship you, write poems for you, fill your life with flowers and joy. Yes. It's all true – I'm a con-man who was going to leave you with nothing, only I found my heart of gold. I'm Jack the Lad who's met his match. I'm Dick Turpin in love… I'm Marie Lloyd, I'm the Duke of York… I'm little Bo Peep, I'm Tom Tom the Piper's Son with a pig under my arm… I'm George Smith with a hat shop and a buttonhole.

ADELAIDE. Stop it.

GEORGE. I'm just laying out my stall – pick out what you fancy and we'll call it truth.

ADELAIDE. Don't. Don't you talk down to me. Who are you to talk down to me? You told me to be proud. And now I am. And no one is ever going to talk down to me again. I thought I was afraid, but I'm not like you. I'm not running away from what I am and playing silly little games so I don't have to notice. I know who I am. I'm Mrs Love.

GEORGE. There is no Mrs Love.

ADELAIDE. Yes there is. I saw her in the mirror last night. You gave her to me and now she's mine. I want to be Mrs Love. I like being Mrs Love. Mrs Love has got nice hands and pretty hair. You can't take her away from me.

GEORGE. I can do what I bloody well like…

ADELAIDE. And so can I. Will you stay with me George?

It is a question, no trace of pleading.

GEORGE. You been reading too many penny romances darling.

ADELAIDE. I don't read penny romances. Will you stay with me?

She waits. He says nothing.

Will you?

He says nothing. She stands looking at him for one moment. Then, she goes to her case, carries it to the bed and opens it… He watches her…

GEORGE. What's this?

ADELAIDE. Is that your real name? Smith? George Smith. And where do you really come from? Stepney? Whitechapel? Bethnal Green?

GEORGE. I never been to Bethnal Green.

She begins slowly to put her things together and pack her case.

ADELAIDE. I helped out at a Christmas soup kitchen in Bethnal Green. Near it anyway. On the corner of Brick Lane. Do you know Brick Lane George? I don't suppose you would if you've never been to Bethnal Green. Lots of little poky houses. All black and filthy and piled together. And the children… you can't think of them as children really. Just things in filthy clothes you don't want to touch. Not worth anything to anyone. Stealing. Telling lies. And running away. George Smith from Bethnal Green. Is that who I was with last night?

She picks up her nightie and looks at it a while. She folds it slowly and carefully. Lays it in her case. Throughout he watches her…

GEORGE. Where are you going?

ADELAIDE. Back to where I was. There is nowhere else is there.

GEORGE. Don't think you can fetch the old bill on to me…

He grabs the money from his pocket.

.

You gave me this fair and square… 'safer in an inside pocket you said. What's mine is yours. Of course you can have it all.'

She goes to her case and closes it. She puts on her coat.

You've got your brooch after all. Your beautiful diamond brooch. Try building your dreams on that. Think I'm soft or something? Leaving behind a hundred quid brooch? Bringing back a hundred quid's worth of diamonds, because of you. It's paste. Paste darling. Rubbish. Half a crown down the market. Not worth the thieving. Your old Auntie got sold short somewhere.

ADELAIDE. I'm going now…

She turns, picks up her case. She moves to the door. He watches her.

GEORGE. Where do you think you're going, hey? Back to your dad. Think he'll have you? He won't you know. A ruined woman… here all night with another man… you won't get much change out of telling him you just played cards… Look, don't go back there. Don't go back there. Have the name. Have it. Keep it. Wear it. Hang it over your hat shop. Make a shroud out of it if you want… Mrs Love, there you are. You're Mrs Love…

She is at the door.

Where are you going?

(It is a desolate cry of panic. It stops her. For a long moment they stand without speaking…

ADELAIDE. What else should I do?

He has no answer.

What do you want me to do?

Silence.

GEORGE. You don't know nothing about me…

ADELAIDE. I know you made me happy for the first time. I know I want to do the same for you. If you'd let me. If you wanted… me to. I know it might be the last hope we have… And you know that too… don't you? Don't you?

For a moment he is held by her. And then he pulls back, finds the money in his pocket.

GEORGE. Have your money.

ADELAIDE. I don't want it.

GEORGE. It's your money…

ADELAIDE. I don't want it…

GEORGE. It's your bloody money.

ADELAIDE. We can love each other.

GEORGE. I don't want your love. I don't need your love…

ADELAIDE. Are you sure? Are you sure George?

GEORGE. I want… I want… I want…

He takes hold of her in an embrace that turns into something else…

What's it going to be? What's it going to be now? The back of the hand, hey? A few slaps, hey? Is that where we go? Happily ever after with the mark of my hand across your face. He doesn't mean it. He can't help it. He loves me. He loves me. I love you Mrs Love. Lock us both up forever with love. Smothering and struggling. Worming in and out. Twisting together like maggots in a tin. Twisted up so you can't tell one from the other, twisted up, clinging on, both go down together. Mrs Love… And some little kid, some little kid you hardly notice… listening, trying to get between us. He doesn't understand, does he? He thinks you love him because he loves you. He doesn't know love's squeezed out of you like blood, it's crushed out of you like juice. – Don't you hurt my mum no more, don't you bloody hurt my mum no more – making stupid little plans – let's run away. I've got two bob saved mum. Let's run away, let's go now. Just you and me. You don't need him no more. And she stands there, looking down at me, my bloody two bob in her hand – that's your father you're talking about you ungrateful little sod… Please… Don't leave me.

ADELAIDE. I won't. I won't. Not ever.

He lets her go. She moves to the table and lights the gas ring. The silence is long.

GEORGE. You make a nice composition standing there. Very sweet. Very nice. I'd paint you if I could. My father was a painter. Did I tell you?

ADELAIDE. No.

GEORGE. An artist. George Thomas… Love R.A. Flowers and Figures. He painted my mother many times. She had this soft rose pink dress and brown hair. So beautiful. She'd read me stories. Rows and rows of story books I had. And toys. Big trunk full of toys. Just for me.

He stops.

Christmas. I was three, my father made me a rocking horse. He made this rocking horse with his own hands, just for me. Dapple grey with polished pine rockers and a real leather bridle with brass fittings. I come down Christmas morning, and there it was. Red ribbon round its neck. Just for me. I got on it there and then. And rode and rode and rode…

ADELAIDE. To where?

GEORGE. Somewhere else.

ADELAIDE. Here you are then… home.

GEORGE. I'll be no good to you.

ADELAIDE. That's for me to say.

GEORGE. You don't know the half of it.

ADELAIDE. I don't need to.

GEORGE. It's cold.

ADELAIDE. I'll turn up the fire.

GEORGE. It's dark, like night.

ADELAIDE. It's raining.

GEORGE. I hate the rain.

ADELAIDE. I'll light the lamp.

GEORGE. No.

ADELAIDE. It's all right.

She does so.

It'll all be all right. We come from the same place you and I, and wherever we go after this it'll be together. Whatever happens… it'll be all right…

She sits beside him.

Think of your favourite dinner. The best thing in the world.

GEORGE. I don't know.

ADELAIDE. There must be something – I make a good Sunday roast. Potatoes done in dripping. Yorkshire pudding in the meat juices. Would you like that? I could cook it for you, one day. What would you like for afters?

Silence.

How about treacle pudding? Steamed treacle pudding... I make a lovely rice pudding too. You got to stir in the skins, that's the secret. Slow cooking and stirring in the skins. Do you like rice pudding?

GEORGE. With jam.

ADELAIDE. Jam spoils a good one, you won't have it with mine. I'll make you jam roll. Soft and sticky. With the jam all oozing out, mixing with the custard... What are you looking at?

GEORGE. You.

ADELAIDE. What for?

GEORGE. I'm thinking you'd make a bloody good brag player.

ADELAIDE. Then teach me. Teach me now.

GEORGE. It takes years.

ADELAIDE. We've got years... haven't we?

GEORGE. Do you like the cinematograph?

ADELAIDE. I've never seen it.

GEORGE. You haven't lived then. They can do anything with moving pictures. I've seen time go backwards.

ADELAIDE. Don't be silly.

GEORGE. Walls falling upwards. Broken jugs mending themselves and all the spilt milk pouring back in.

ADELAIDE. Really?

GEORGE. You can be sitting in the dark and there's a train rushing at you out of the wall. Some people scream. Reallest thing they've ever seen.

ADELAIDE. You'll have to take me.

GEORGE. Only the thing is – it's not there. You can put your hand through it, turn the light up – and it's gone. It's just a bit of smoke. A bit of nothing at all.

ADELAIDE. Best to keep the lights down then.

Pause.

Is it paste? Did you leave my brooch because it was paste?

GEORGE. No. It's as real as anything you'll ever know.

ADELAIDE. Really?

GEORGE. Really.

She takes off her coat and puts away her things, as she does so she sings almost to herself.

I'LL BE YOUR SWEETHEART
IF YOU WILL BE MINE
ALL MY LIFE
I'LL BE YOUR VALENTINE
BLUEBELLS I'LL GATHER
TAKE THEM AND BE TRUE
WHEN I'M A MAN…
MY PLAN WILL BE TO MARRY YOU…

Pause.

Things are what we make them. That's what Rose says… It might be true. Mightn't it?

Your bath's getting cold.

ADELAIDE. My bath?

GEORGE. Mustn't waste the hot.

ADELAIDE. I suppose not.

GEORGE. I could soap you down.

ADELAIDE. Yes. I've got a nice bit of lavender soap – in my bag. Lovely soft lather.

GEORGE. Then you could get dry by the fire. Put your scent on.

He touches where he'd apply it.

Then you could put on your new nightie… and go to bed. If you'd like that.

ADELAIDE. I'd like that… I'll get ready then.

She takes off her brooch and holds it out to him. After a moment he takes it from her. She begins to undo her dress buttons. She takes off her dress.

Will you undo the laces?

He begins to do so.

Her laces undone she steps out of her top layers and stands before him.

I feel self-conscious.

GEORGE. No you don't, you know just what you are. You're beautiful. And clever. And strong. And the best thing that ever happened to me.

She looks up at him for a moment. She kisses him.

ADELAIDE. I'll go and get in the bath then.

GEORGE. You don't have to.

ADELAIDE. I know that…

She moves away into the darkness.

GEORGE. I'll soap you down… starting at your feet and working up… slowly up and up… rinse you down… rub you dry by the fire…

He reaches out into nothing, touching perfume onto a body only he can see…

Then you'll put on your new nightie… you'll look so lovely in it… and we'll go to bed… and keep each other warm, and talk about tomorrow…

He turns to look out front.

She got in. I stood in front of her, looking down at her. I picked up the soap and rubbed it between my palms until the lather dripped and ran into the water. I thought about soaping her down… starting at her feet and working slowly up and up… I thought about it… And then I reached out and touched her cheek. She looked up at me for a moment and smiled. It's all right George. It's all right now. Yes, I said. And kissed her… And drew my hand over her skin. Then I took hold of her under the chin… and pushed her face under the water. She struggled. Just a bit. Just a little bit. But I'm strong. And it was no trouble. After a while she was still. And that was it really.

THE END

www.ingramcontent.com/pod-product-compliance
Lightning Source LLC
LaVergne TN
LVHW051806080426
835511LV00019B/3416